DATE DUE

SE 16 '03	Amanda	8-116	
FE 0 2 06	Moe	103	
MR 2 3 '06	Gabriel M.	1/	
AP 17 '08	Carlos B	103	
AP 08 '09	Jake	116	

DEMCO 38-296

OFF TO THE RACES

PETER & NILDA SESSLER

The Rourke Press, Inc.
Vero Beach, Florida 32964

PHOTO CREDITS
© Chevrolet: pages 4, 13, 18, 19, 21, 22; © Chrysler Coporation: page 7; © Pennzoil Company: cover; © Peter Sessler: pages 6, 9, 10, 15, 16; © Raceway Park: page 12

EDITORIAL SERVICES:
Susan Albury

Library of Congress Cataloging-in-Publication Data

Sessler, Peter C., 1950-
   Drag cars / Peter Sessler, Nilda Sessler.
      p. cm. — (Off to the races)
   Includes index.
   Summary: Describes the nature and rules of drag racing and the special characteristics of drag cars.
   ISBN 1-57103-280-0
   1. Drag racing Juvenile literature. 2. Dragsters Juvenile literature.
[1. Drag racing. 2. Automobiles, Racing.] I. Sessler, Nilda, 1951- . II. Title.
III. Series: Sessler, Peter C., 1950- Off to the races.
GV1029.3.S47 1999
796.72—dc21   99-13824
                                                              CIP

Printed in the USA

■ TABLE OF CONTENTS

◼◻◻ WHAT IS DRAG RACING?

Drag racing is one of the most unusual types of racing. The races are very short because the distance covered is only 1/4 mile. Drag racing developed as a result of young people racing their cars on city streets and highways in the 1930s and 1940s. They would "drag" it out to see who was fastest.

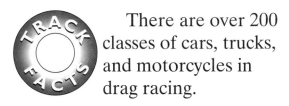 There are over 200 classes of cars, trucks, and motorcycles in drag racing.

The most powerful racing cars on Earth are drag racers, reaching speeds of over 300 miles per hour in just over 4-1/2 seconds.

■■ DRAG RACING RULES

The NHRA (National Hot Rod Association), AHRA (American Hot Rod Association), and IHRA (International Hot Rod Association) make the rules for drag racing. There are over 200 types or classes of cars that race.

Some cars have engines in the front, some behind the driver, some cars are built from scratch, and some are just like the ones you see driving on the road. At one time, there were drag cars that had two engines!

Even though drag cars are incredibly fast, they are very safe because of the strict rules that have to be followed by every racer.

Safety rules are very important in drag racing. Special steel tubes surround the driver for protection. Notice the tiny steering wheel and the shifter, which is in the middle of the floor.

■■ A WORD FROM OUR SPONSOR

Almost no one can afford to race without the help from sponsors because racing has become very expensive. It can cost millions of dollars to run one of the top teams today. The sponsors help to pay the cost of running the teams and so they get to put their names and logos on the cars.

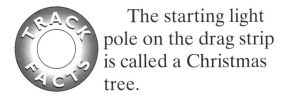 The starting light pole on the drag strip is called a Christmas tree.

Racing is very expensive, so many cars have sponsors who help pay for the car. This funny car's main sponsor is Kendall Oil Co.

◪ THE STRIP

The drag racing track is called a drag strip. It has two lanes and the distance from the starting line to the finish line is only 1/4 mile or 1,320 feet. The lanes continue for another 1/4 mile to 1/2 mile, so speeding cars have room to slow down.

The drag strip at Raceway Park in Englishtown, NJ. Races here are held during the day and at night.

At the starting line of the strip is a light called a "Christmas Tree." When the light turns green, the cars go!

Some drag strips are even smaller. The distance from the start to the finish line is only 1/8 of a mile, or 660 feet. Each track has stands alongside the strip for people to watch and cheer. There is also space for a garage where the mechanics work on the cars.

THE ROARING CARS

There are many types of drag racing cars. The most powerful and fastest are the top fuel dragsters. The sounds they make are almost frightening and shake your whole body. Dragsters have supercharged engines that produce over 6,000 horsepower. A supercharger forces extra fuel into the engine so it makes more power. The fuel they use is called **nitromethane** (ni tro METH ane) and in one 1/4 mile race, over 20 gallons are used!

 The fuel used on top fuel dragsters and funny cars, nitromethane, is a combination of nitric acid and propane.

An unusual drag racer is this jet-powered limo. It sounds like a jet plane taking off!

The fastest top fuel dragsters can do the 1/4 mile in four and a half seconds and reach speeds of over 300 miles per hour. That's as fast as counting one and two and three and four and reaching the finish line!

Just as exciting, and only about 1/2 a second slower, are the **funny cars** (FUN nee karz). Back in 1964 when they first raced, someone said, "Boy, these cars look funny!" and the name stuck. Funny cars look like regular cars but their bodies are just **fiberglass** (fi bur GLAS) shells that fit over a metal tube frame.

Here the mechanics are working on a top fuel dragster. Notice the two silver bundles between the rear tires. They are the parachutes that slow it down at the end of the race.

◼️ ELIMINATION TIME

For the big national races, the cars always arrive at the track a few days before the races begin. Even though all the tracks look the same, each one is different. The temperature, humidity, and different types of pavement affect how the cars run. The drivers take time to practice on the track so they can get to know how their cars will run on the drag strip. The mechanics also go over the cars to make sure everything is working perfectly.

Before racing down the strip, the cars warm up the tires by doing burnouts, which make lots of smoke.

The green light is on and this truck is on its way down the strip doing a "Wheelie"—that's when the front wheels lift of the ground.

When race day finally comes, the cars that are in the same class are paired. Each pair of cars race each other and the losing one is eliminated from further racing. These are called elimination races. Then, all the winning cars are paired against each other until there are only two cars left. In the final race, the two fastest cars race against each other. The winner is called the **Top Eliminator** (TOP ee LIM ah nay tor).

Other classes of cars race against each other in the same way. This may take two to three days and is very exciting. The winner gets a trophy and prize money.

The drag strips are usually open during most of the year so local racers can race. The big name racers may not be there but the racing action is just as exciting.

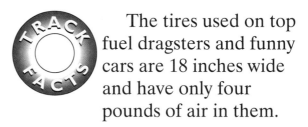 The tires used on top fuel dragsters and funny cars are 18 inches wide and have only four pounds of air in them.

Without parachutes to slow it down at the end of the race, this racer could have a serious accident.

◩ GLOSSARY

accelerate (ak SEL er rate) — to move as quickly as possible

drag strip (DRAG strip) — a strip of pavement with a racing area at least 1/4 mile long, where drag racing takes place

fiberglass (fi bur GLAS) — material made of fine threads of glass

funny cars (FUN nee karz) — a specialized dragster that has a one-piece molded body

nitromethane (ni tro METH ane) — a liquid chemical used as fuel for dragsters and funny cars

top eliminator (TOP ee LIM ah nay tor) — the winner of the final elimination race

CONVERSION TABLE

1/4 mile	402 meters	660 feet	201 meters
1,320 feet	402 meters	20 gallons	76 liters
1/2 mile	805 meters	300 miles per hour	483 kilometers per hour
1/8 mile	201 meters		

The winner gets prize money and a trophy. This is Tom Hammonds.

◾️ INDEX

FURTHER READING

Find out more about racing with these helpful books and organizations:

• Martin Hintz & Kate Hintz, *Top Fuel Drag Racing.* 1998

• Jeff Savage, *Drag Racing.* 1996

• NHRA's Official Site: www.nhra.com

• IHRA's Home Site: www.ihra.com

• www.goracing.com

   Lots of information on all types of racing. The site also posts racing schedules and results of every race.